# UNDERSTANDING
# BIBLICAL
# FAITH

## M. Alan Miller, PhD

WESTBOW
P R E S S®
A DIVISION OF THOMAS NELSON
& ZONDERVAN

WestBow Press books may be ordered through booksellers or by contacting:

WestBow Press
A Division of Thomas Nelson & Zondervan
1663 Liberty Drive
Bloomington, IN 47403
www.westbowpress.com
844-714-3454

ISBN: 978-1-6642-9388-5 (sc)
ISBN: 978-1-6642-9389-2 (e)

Library of Congress Control Number: 2023904082

Print information available on the last page.

WestBow Press rev. date: 03/13/2023

# FAITH: "WHAT'S IT ALL ABOUT, ALFIE?"

The 1966 song written by Burt Bacharach for the British comedy-drama movie "Alfie," was popularized in the U.S. by superb song stylist, Dionne Warwick (See lyrics at end). The words clearly depict a person at a crossroads searching earnestly for the meaning of life. As born-again believers you and I know that the person simply needs to turn his/her life over to Jesus, who is the Life of God (John 14:6) and that through <u>faith</u> in Him the seeker will be made into a new creation through His indwelling Spirit, become right with God, have a personal relationship with Him, walk with Him through this life, and be destined to join Him in eternity at physical death.

# INTRODUCTION

Faith is at the same time a simple yet profound topic. Through its simplicity it *can* secure salvation and a modest amount of spiritual growth but if we are to move on to maturity we must get a firm grip on exactly what faith is as well as what it isn't. If that is your sincere desire, I encourage you to continue reading and join me in an exploratory journey that promises to take us to new heights in our walk with Christ Jesus.

Along the way you will undoubtedly come across points in this study that will bring to mind possible contradictions with your concept of faith, so I encourage you to keep an open mind and search out a particular verse in the Appendix that you think contradicts the point in question. There you will find relevant verses in order of appearance in the Bible (New American Standard translation) then read the commentary that follows which explains how it may not contradict to the point being made.

Example:   **Study point** – you will <u>not</u> receive additional faith.
**Appendix verse** – Matthew 17:20 read the commentary

The term "faith" is one that is tossed about lightly as if everyone knows what it means. In fact, other than saving faith, the topic itself is seldom preached or taught leaving it up to us to create our own interpretation of the many facets of its meaning and use. I think that you will agree that it is the key to not only favor with God but for our individual Christian walk, so it behooves each of us to carefully excavate the deep meaning of faith from the rich soil of God's Word. And as we become thoroughly knowledgeable about it we will then be able to execute it properly and walk confidently in its path. (Hebrews 11:1c, 2 Timothy 3:17)

To begin our faith exploration, let us agree on three general faith terms:

√ The faith: a belief system stemming from the life and teachings of Jesus of Nazareth (the Christ/Messiah) i.e. the Christian faith as opposed to others
√ Faith, a relational faculty that all Christian believers possess and may exercise for putting their confidence in Jesus and His Truths
√ The spiritual gift of faith/faithfulness allotted exclusively to a select few believers through whom God can display his power

A deep dive into the Biblical concept of faith is a complex undertaking, and if you have never taken the plunge I can assure you that if you are like most believers you will find it somewhat to very different from what you now perceive it to be. If you are typical, what you think you know about the nature of faith will be severely challenged and you will be reluctant to give up your long-held assumptions about it. This study will not rely on persuasion but on solid Biblical proof and it may not even be until near the end that you will completely buy into what God lays out in His Word about this key element of Christian Truth.

# PREVIEW

By way of a preview allow me to expose you to a few of the topics that will be covered in much more detail (along with Biblical support) in the body of the study:

- Faith has a precise Biblical meaning and it is not up to believers to define it.
- Faith must be based on Truth.
- A Biblically accurate acronym for faith is "Fully Anticipating It To Happen."
- Faith is the ONLY way to please God.
- Faith, belief, and trust have overlapping but separate meanings.
- Faith is a "knowing" about the result of the faith that we exercise, not a wishing.
- Faith is not unsubstantial because God says that it IS substance.
- He also says that faith, not the result of it, is evidence.
- God expects us to know what faith is and exercise it accurately in our daily lives.
- Faith is designed to & will overcome your self, the world around you, and our enemy.
- Faith is the way we are supposed to walk every moment of every day.

- Faith is a spirit-world resource to be exercised in the physical world for God's purposes, our good, and the good of others.
- Your faith walk is a testimony and encouragement to others.
- The prayer of faith is only one of many types of prayer in the Bible.
- Unlike the New Testament Koine Greek, our English does not have a verb form for "faith" and that causes us English speakers much difficulty in fully grasping what our various Bible translations say about it.
- Faith is a definitional issue and has nothing to do with the amount that we possess.
- Jesus tells us that faith, properly exercised, can and will move a mountain.
- Accurately applied, faith achieves its end every time.
- Avoid controversies about faith since the faith of the believer works!
- Everything apart from faith is sin! (Yes, the Bible says so)
- Faith is a relational faculty, to be sure, but in our day-to-day lives it is a choice e.g. "Will I trust the Lord and His Word in this or not?"
- God may call us to act through faith without understanding.
- Faith allows God's will to be transferred out of heaven.
- The faith of a believer will be tested but it does produce perseverance, fruit, and a good testimony, etc. James 1:3, 1Peter 1: 7b
- Faith overcomes the flesh, the world, and our enemy.

# FAITH IS THE KEY TO PLEASING GOD

In Hebrews 11, which is commonly called "God's Hall of Faith," it says in verse 2 that those named in the passage "obtained a good report." [i.e. were commended, gained approval, were pleasing to God, etc.] According to Matthew Henry, "Faith always has been the mark of God's servants, from the beginning of the world." From a human standpoint, if we asked someone to do something, we would be interested in seeing if they did it and then commended them for their action. However, it will not come as a shock to you to consider that God does not operate as we do. We know that He is omniscient (all knowing) and His omniscience is not bound by time and space as we are. Even before He gives a command/promise to someone He already knows that they will exercise faith and obey, so in effect He could issue the good report even before the person applies faith and obeys. He knew full well that they would act under the influence of faith. The only reason I say this is that I want you to begin thinking from God's perspective as we move through the study. Let's take Abram for instance. This takes us back to a time when there were no Scriptures and, since He was the first Jew there was no tribe of Israel. Abram was reportedly from the tenth generation after Noah and lived in the Sumerian region in

Ur where the people were polytheistic. God spoke directly to Abram and there is no record of his being awestruck by this but we simply do not know His reaction. At any rate we realize that Abram somehow knew Who was speaking so he listened, received his marching orders, and exercised faith by setting out on the journey called for by God. While we are impressed, Abram's calling is no different or better than the callings that you and I receive as we walk with God by faith. Just as **we** know God I believe it safe to infer that Abram also knew Him and that He was faithful. (1 Corinthians 1:9) So the question becomes for you and me since we know God, are we always listening and prepared to hear and obey? [He certainly always knows where we are spiritually.]

[A theatrical aside: While we are on the subject of Abraham, let's take a sneak peak at a particularly knotty problem that will be explored in more detail later. Question: Does Romans 4:3 say that Abraham believed God or believed in God and it was credited to him as righteousness? Let's face it, sadly most of the converts through the ministry of our churches are our own children (and not even all of those). So when a child hears the appeal to believe in Jesus is it not reasonable to expect that child to mix it with similar appeals to believe in Santa Claus, the Easter bunny, the tooth fairy, etc. For 32 years that was my mindset for believing in Jesus. I unshakably believed that He was born of a virgin, had lived a perfect life, taught, healed, raised the dead, was crucified, died for everyone's sins, was buried in a cave, was resurrected, spent 40 days on earth before His ascension, and was seated at the right hand of His Father. But, did my belief save me? Oh my no!!!!!, even our enemy believes all that and more. I say all this to make the point that we need to be super adept at how we speak about all Biblical issues and especially faith because of its complexities. More about this later.]

# WHY AREN'T ALL OF MY PRAYERS ANSWERED?

If you have been a believer for a while you have learned that some things you have trusted God for came to pass while others did not, right? Of course those that did not could be the result of not being according to His will and/or because of unconfessed sin standing between you and Him. So a preface to any prayer request should always be to ask the Lord to reveal any active sin in your life. John 16:8 tells us that the Holy Spirit's responsibility is to convict of sin, and righteousness, and judgment. So, if we ask this, we can depend on Him to bring our sins to mind so that we may ask for forgiveness. Once we have asked the Lord to forgive us of that/those sin/sins then we are assured by 1John 1:9 that God is faithful and righteous to forgive us our sins and cleanse us of all unrighteousness. Now that we are cleansed, the next step is to ask Him to fill us with His Holy Spirit, At that point the path is clear for our request. But even then the Lord may respond with one of three responses: Yes, no, or wait. (Keep in mind that His timing and ours may not be the same – we know that Abraham waited 25 years for Isaac and David waited 15 years to be crowned king). So, an important point to keep in mind is that He has a plan/path for you and me and He may have disapproved our request because we have "asked amiss." (See James 4:3) The sad part of unanswered prayer is that a believer may begin to doubt – doubt salvation, doubt the Lord's love, doubt having "enough" faith, doubt worthiness, etc. James 1:6c tells us that: "the one who doubts is like a wave of the sea that is driven and tossed by the wind." And, indeed, doubt can hinder our prayers (See Matthew 14:31, 21:21, Mark 11:23, Luke 24:38, John 20:27, Romans 14:23, James 1:5-8, etc.) In the final analysis, upon what was our prayer based? Most likely an unanswered prayer may be based on our own will not God's. [stay tuned]

# FAITH CONNECTS ME TO GOD'S WILL

Consider this: Faith is embedded within the believer as a direct connection to God's will. It allows us to tap into His will much as household appliances tap into the electrical grid. It is a God-given resource and cannot be conjured up by one's mind, will, or emotion. Each of us has the same quantity of faith which will not be increased or diminished. (Matthew 17:20) But our faith may grow qualitatively as we exercise it properly according to 2 Corinthians 10:15b "...*with the hope that as your faith grows...*" [See also 2 Thessalonians 1:3, Romans 4:20) Obviously sin, disobedience, and unbelief will hinder or negate it. It is not powerful in itself but connects us to God's will and He is the One with the power to bring it about for or through the believer. When initiated, it is in effect a transaction between us and God Himself. Productive faith is accomplished in one of two ways: by a petition/intercession which is consistent with God's will or by hearing from God and laying claim to what He reveals through His Word or His Spirit.

As you know, faith is not restricted to those with born-again status since Abel, Enoch, Noah, Abraham and many other Old Testament saints heard from God and obeyed. This is in contrast to Adam, Cain, and many others who heard from God and yet disobeyed.

# WHAT ARE YOUR THOUGHTS ABOUT FAITH?

Job lived around 2200 years before Christ and was thought to be a contemporary of Abraham, Lot, and Isaac. He knew well that "the Lord gives and the Lord takes away" (Job 1:21) and so will it be with you in this study. The Lord is going to give you new insights into the true meaning and exercise of faith as well as take away some of what you have always thought you understood about it as well as correct any past incorrect practices of faith. So let's dive right in and explore the first part of God's precise definition of faith in Hebrews 11:1 "Now faith is the <u>substance</u> of things hoped for..." So, first of all, God is saying that faith is <u>not</u> incorporeal (i.e. has no material form). He is saying that faith itself **IS** substance. Our problem is that we were born into and lived a few years before our salvation totally isolated in a physical existence [our mom our crib, our food, and everything around us]. So we naturally identified everything as substance. We were born as physical beings with physical eyes, ears, and brain so when we used them to look around during the years before our rebirth and identified everything in sight as substance, consequently we bought into the lie that "seeing is believing." And since we cannot see, touch or hear faith we must take "by faith" God's extraordinary assertion of it as substance.

Next let us explore the differences among the terms of belief, faith, and trust. With regard to belief, let us agree that our minds are filled with a multitude of beliefs but as we constantly discover not all of them are true, and very few involve faith or trust. So we can conclude that faith and trust are much narrower concepts than belief since we do not necessarily trust or have faith in everything we believe. For instance, we might believe that we could safely cross a particular swinging bridge or pond of ice but might not trust them because of the possible risks involved in doing so. So whereas a belief is a set of ideas that at any point of time we hold to be true (a mental construct), trust and faith are active reliances upon something or someone in whom we have confidence. Obviously we do not trust or have faith in everything we believe to exist. And finally, let us begin to understand that trust is also a more general term than belief since we know from experience that some things/persons we have trusted have not been worthy of that trust. We may have trusted an old ladder only to have one of the rungs break and cause us to fall to the ground. Now let's move on to the most narrow of the three: faith. In order to exercise faith it must be based on something or Someone that is true/Truth and the 3 Truths that we know are **Jesus** (John 14:6), **His Spirit** (John 16:13), and **God's Word** (John 17:17),

As you know, trust can be either a noun or a verb since we can trust (verb) something/ someone or have trust in that thing/person (noun). Sadly, our English language does not have a verb form for "faith." but In both Koine Greek and Aramaic, faith has both noun and verb forms. So the translators into English are hamstrung into translating the faith word as "trust" or more commonly "believe" or even worse, "believe in." In addition, in the Hebrew Old Testament the concept of faith is not used much as a noun at all, but it is used more as a verb: (Genesis 15:6 "And Abram believed Jehovah and this was accounted for him as righteousness". Many English translations read "believed in" but the word "in" is not in the original language) *refer back to the earlier discussion of "believe vs believe in."* Note that since Abraham's "believing" Jehovah was accounted to him as righteousness it was based on the Truths that God had spoken to him making a more accurate translation that of "faith." If you are with me in this insight then please indulge me in this study when I often use faith as a verb.

With regard to faith needing to be based on Truth, accept this helpful acronym for faith as "**F**ully **A**nticipating **I**t **T**o **H**appen." Oral Roberts, who founded Oral Roberts University in Tulsa, often said on his Sunday morning tv show: "I know because I know because I know." In effect he was conveying that his "knowing" was absolutely True since it was based on God's Truth.

**REVIEW:** Belief and believing are more general terms than either trust/trusting or faith. At one extreme a belief can be superficial, shallow, and trivial like believing in the Easter Bunny while at the other extreme it can involve total commitment like to our mom, our athletic team/coach, our country, etc. Whereas belief is a mental structure, trust involves a reliance on something or someone even if not trustworthy. Finally, <u>faith</u> is an absolutely concrete "knowing' about the outcome since it is based on God's Truth. For the purpose of our study we will use faith as both a noun and verb in order to make our focus clear.

# FAITH – SECULAR VS SPIRITUAL

An important issue regarding the term faith is that it exists in both a secular form as well as a Biblical form. The secular variety can be applied to anything or anyone whereas the Biblical variety, as we have seen, is limited to being based on God's Truth. (This thought will be developed further as we go along.) The way I think of these is lower case "f" faith and upper case "F" faith. [As you will see later, the same view applies to secular and Biblical "hope."] When you read Matthew 21:22 it would be easy to become disenchanted with the Truth of God's Word without knowing the Koine Greek meaning behind the word "believing." "And whatever you ask in prayer, believing, you will receive it all". The word "believing" would be correctly translated "faithing," if English had such a word. So if a nonbeliever is the one doing the "asking" or if a believer asked amiss (John 4:3) obviously God has not obligated Himself to honor the request except in the case of the nonbeliever "faithing" Him for salvation. As we have seen, this word in the Greek is the gerand form of the Greek word for faith and, as we have seen, must be connected to Truth which only comes from God. So, if you ask for anything in prayer that is according to something that God has promised you will indeed receive it. For example if in your morning quiet time with the Lord you ask Him to help you not to be timid today but go forth with power and love and discipline you will have it,. And why? Because God promised it in 2 Timothy 1:7 "For God has not given us a spirit of timidity, but of power and love and discipline." [According to an Internet source there are over 3,000 promises in the Bible]

Maybe without realizing it, when the Spirit of Jesus came to reside within you and me we received a new resource since beginning at that point we had access to His eyes (spiritual sight) based on His Truth. So, in effect, we now had a choice to make at each point in our lives between what we saw with our physical eyes and what we saw with the spiritual eyes within us. If what we see with these two conflict then the correct choice is always in the spiritual realm by faith, which **IS** substance. [2 Corinthians 5:7 "...for we walk by faith, not by sight..." and this verse explains that trying to walk using your physical eyes does not reveal True substance. [I hope that this is clear.] So our life-long pursuit is that of discerning how to use our spiritual eyes within us and always favoring them over our physical ones.

# GOD'S DEFINITION OF FAITH: PART II

Backing up to the Hebrews 11:1 verse, the second word of interest in God's definition of faith is that of "evidence." Obviously "things unseen" means that we cannot see it with our physical eyes so the Lord is directing us to the spiritual world which is the sphere where True/real things reside. Here we are to understand that what we see/hear with our spiritual eyes/ears is what is authentic. God tells us in Ephesians 2:6 that He has seated us with Christ in the heavens. (Reckon it so!!!) In the human courtroom there is hard evidence as well as circumstantial evidence. The latter requires an inference from human logic but since we are to walk in the spiritual realm by faith we can dismiss this as what the verse means. The evidence in God's courtroom must be absolute Truth, meaning that the verse is obviously speaking of the hard-evidence variety even though it would not be visible with physical eyes. And, what is harder evidence than God's Word? 2 Corinthians 4:18 tells us: "...while we look not at the things which are seen, but at the things which are not seen; for the things which are seen are temporal, but the things which are not seen are eternal." For example, King David **saw** with His spiritual eyes the design of God's temple, drew up the blueprints, and passed them along to his son, Solomon, because God would not permit David to build it since he had "shed much blood." (1 Chronicles 22:8)

**REVIEW:** faith has a precise Biblical meaning which is clearly defined in this study. Faith, while not seen with our physical eyes, is substance and evidence. Our responsibility as born-again believers is to learn to look beyond the temporal things we see with our physical eyes by utilizing our spiritual eyes to see what is revealed by God as eternal and authentic.

Now, to expand on what has been covered: Faith is the confidence, assurance, reality, substance, certainty, conviction, proof, and existence of things hoped for...the conviction, assurance, evidence, and certainty of things not seen. (These are the various descriptive words used in popular Bible translations and hopefully they will clear up any lingering questions about what faith is.)

Next, let's turn our attention to what faith is **not**:

It is not the enemy of reason!

It is not superstition!

It is not wishful thinking!

It is not make-believe! [Make-believe is making yourself believe.]

It is not developing a positive attitude in order to get your way!!

It is not forcing God to go along with your wishes!

It is not "name it and claim it"!

It is not an emotional process!

It is not the opposite of knowledge!

It is not an emotional exercise!

And as our pastor recently put it, "Faith is not a leap into the dark but a leap into the Light!"

# TWO WORLDS: ONE TRUE & ONE COUNTERFEIT FAITH

Romans 12:2 says: "*And do not be conformed to this world, but be transformed by the renewing of your mind, so that you may prove what the will of God is, that which is good and acceptable and perfect.*" From this verse it is implied that what is in the physical world around us is imperfect. We know that God is perfect and He has placed that same perfection within us and He expects us to choose to use the perfect eyes/ears of the Spirit within to discern His will for each and every moment. It is said that the U.S. Treasury Department does <u>not</u> train its agents by having them study counterfeit bills but legitimate ones. So it is supposed to be in our walk, focusing on what is True. And who is True/Truth? Jesus said to Thomas: ",,,I am the Way and the **Truth** and the Life…" (John 14:6) And what the Lord says and has said <u>IS</u> TRUTH as He tells us through King David in Psalm 119:60 a "The sum of Your Word is Truth…"

Remember, in God's definition of faith He says that faith is the substance of things <u>hoped</u> for so let us make it clear that like faith there is human inborn hope and there is Biblical hope. And as with faith I think of human hope as little "h" hope and that kind of hope might or not come about but Biblical hope (capital "H") is based on a confident expectation of what God has said or promised for the "prayed up" believer. Biblical hope has as its foundation faith in God, including what He says in His written Word and though His Spirit. As we know, inborn hope carries with it a measure of doubt. However In both the Old and New Testaments hope and its cognates have the meaning of confidence, security, and being without doubt; therefore, the concept of doubt has no part in the hope (or faith) of believers. Therefore, again, Biblical hope is a confident expectation or assurance based upon a sure foundation for that which we wait with joy and full confidence. Are there any promises made by God in His Word that He did not keep? Rest assured, He is still in the business of promise keeping today and depends on us to take Him at His Word and claim His promises.

**Fact**: Jesus when He was in human form knew what to do every moment because He stayed connected with the Father through faith and reliance upon Him. Brother Lawrence challenges us down through time to "Practice the Presence." [*As a humble cook, Brother Lawrence learned an important lesson through each daily chore: He believed that the time he spent in communion with his Lord should be the same, whether he was bustling around in the kitchen—with several people asking questions at the same time—or on his knees in prayer.*]

# THE SOURCE OF BIBLICAL FAITH

"Faith comes from hearing and hearing comes from the Word of God". (Romans 10:17) And where does God speak? (through the Bible and through His Spirit and not necessarily through circumstances) This may be controversial but it seems to me that "believing" is accomplished in our soul (mind, will, and emotions) whereas "faithing" is performed in our spirit, apart from our soul. (Koine Greek: noun for faith = *pistis*; verb for faith = *pisteuo* - in other words from the same root. And through what God says to us begins to change our will, our ways, our affections, our objections, and even our disposition. He offers us new purpose and new goals. As we learn from Him we agree with God about being out of step with Him (sinning) and desire to conform to His will and ways. We simply confess, receive forgiveness, and walk forward with Him, faithing Him to change us from the inside out. Our hands/feet/mind/will/emotions/ affections are planted in the physical world while He has, according to Ephesians 2:6, spiritually "...seated us with Him in the heavenly *places* in Christ Jesus." [Since our life and identity is in Christ, as He sits in the heavenly places, so do we. "In the heavenly places" is where our blessings are and where we have fellowship with the Father, the Son, the Holy Spirit, so when we are "prayed up" and are in communion with God this is when we are in those "heavenly places." In other words, in communion with Him we are transported to where He is. [*Why is it that we seem to find it easier to wrap our heads around being buried with Christ in baptism than perceiving ourselves as being seated with Him in the heavenly places when we are in direct fellowship with Him. If God said it, we need to embrace it!*]

# WHAT DOES GOD EXPECT OF ME?

What has always been God's expectation for man? To be holy! (Leviticus 11:44-45, Leviticus 19:2, 20:7, 20:26, 21:8, Deuteronomy 23:14, 1 Peter 1:15-16, Hebrews 12:14, etc.) But, as you well know, since we have retained our old nature (flesh) we cannot have holy behavior on our own. Our only claim to holiness is the Spirit of Jesus within us since new birth. Abraham was declared to be righteous yet not holy. When the Father looks down upon the born again believer He sees the righteousness, the holiness, and the perfection of His Son within and that should cause us to SHOUT "HALLELUJAH!"! He is so pleased with His Son that His pleasure carries over to you and to me. (Hebrews10: 14 "For by one offering He has perfected for all time those who are sanctified".) And this, of course, has nothing to do with our fallen feelings about ourselves. But it is a rock-solid Biblical fact! Of course our behavior will seldom match those lofty adjectives "until that day" (2 Timothy 1:12) but we can live by faith in the meantime. So let's roll up our sleeves and learn how.

The Greek word used for **holy** or holiness is "*hagios*" and means much the same thing as the Old Testament word "*godesh*" which means "pure, morally blameless," or "set apart" as in set apart for holy use, which is what we saints of God have been called to. And, of course, the only way we as believers can lay claim to holiness is through the holiness of Jesus who dwells within us.

Being **perfect** is having never sinned. Again, Christ in us is our perfection and through His presence we are "made perfect". (Hebrews 10:14).

Being **righteous** is simply being right with God, which we are from our receipt of Jesus as our Savior and Lord.

Jesus is and has always been holy, perfect, and righteous whereas Abram in his day was only righteous because God declared Him to be so. While you and I in Christ are seen by God to be holy, perfect, and righteous He does not yet see perfect behavior. While we agonize over this we also need to rejoice over what God sees in us and continue to grow/mature in Christ. So, lighten up on yourself and steadfastly point your ship toward its prescribed destination: being like Christ.

> **Bonus:** Beyond being saved and bringing our moment-by-moment thoughts, words and actions in line with God's expectations there are huge accompanying benefits: Isaiah 32:17 "The fruit of righteousness will be peace; the effect of righteousness will be quietness and confidence forever".

The following command seems impossible so we may tend to want to write it off by rationalizing "surely He doesn't expect that of me." 2 Corinthians 10:5c – "...take every thought captive to obey Christ." And, of course, thoughts lead to words and actions. Can we admit that almost everything about our behavior is sin? (Romans 14:23) But, remember there is forgiveness just a prayer away (1 John 1:9).

**REVIEW:** Accept the FACT that you, through Christ Jesus, ARE holy, perfect, and righteous in our relationship with God, even though our behavior falls short. Keep this deposited in the bank but continue BY FAITH to hone your behavior in order to little-by-little live up to the standard that our Lord has set. Accept setbacks and failures but get up, ask for forgiveness, dust yourself off, walk in the Spirit, and stay in the battle since we have a lot of enemies: our own flesh (old man); rulers, authorities, and powers of this dark world; and spiritual forces of evil in the heavenly realms (Ephesians 6:12).

You and I have heard and maybe even said, "if I just had more faith". But remember, as we saw earlier, what Jesus told His disciples in Matthew 17 when they complained about not being able to heal the boy with seizures: "...because of your unbelief" (which literally is "your unfaith"). Since He **is** the Truth (John 14:6) and as Truth He spoke Truth to them when He instructed them to go forth and heal, they obviously did not "faith" His word to them and failed. [And ironically this was right after He was transfigured and the Father had said: "This is My beloved Son, with whom I am well pleased".]

Jesus followed up His rebuke of their unbelief by pointing out that: "...if you have faith the size of a mustard seed, you will say to this mountain, 'Move from here to there,' and it will move; and nothing will be impossible for you." (Matthew 17:20) FAITH WORKS EVERY TIME IT IS PROPERLY APPLIED!!!!! Jesus is assuring you and me through His Word that we never have need for more faith but to simply exercise it, and as we do this our faith will grow like a muscle (2 Thessalonians 1:3). Faith then is claiming a Word from God and acting in a way that demonstrates that we know that He will bring it to pass because of the rock-solid basis for our faith (i.e. Truth). And James teaches us that faith is not an inactive, internal mechanism but requires our corresponding action. James calls it something that we tend to shy away from: "works." (James 2:26) Remember the lepers who were "healed as they went?" (Luke 17:14) Jesus said, "go" and they stepped out in faith based upon Jesus' Word. And, as we are learning, God never expects us to exercise faith and act without a word from Him; and understanding follows that action.

# SELF CHECK

[Matthew 17:20] Ok, if you are still questioning aspects of what we are learning about faith, please pay close attention because there is a lot to learn from the interchange about mustard seed faith between Jesus and His disciples. First of all, put yourself in their shoes: three of them had just witnessed Jesus' transfiguration and had, no doubt, shared that with the others but none of them grasped what that had to do with them. He had shown them His divine majesty and was now giving them the authority to access God's power to do something this remarkable, and yet they did not feel adequate to exercise this faith that He was describing since they saw themselves as poor, powerless young men in a conquered land. Instead of responding to what He (*who is Truth*) was allowing (*which was and is Truth*) they were content to continue to act with their own insignificance/strength which would be destined to fail. And responding to God's promises and commands with the flesh will fail in God's and the world's eyes every time. From the verse we can see that faith taps into the absolute power of God and is clearly designed to work every time it is exercised because it is based upon Truth in the spiritual realm instead of anything in the physical world. [Let us never mistake the faith available to us as our capability but a conduit to God's.]

So faith is a quality issue and not one of quantity. In Romans 4:20 Paul admonishes readers to grow strong in faith, not to request more since faith is like a physical muscle which only grows with exercise. As mentioned earlier, faith provides access to God's POWER and because of the Truth we base it on it WILL happen. What Jesus is saying in His "move a mountain" statement is a hypothetical situation but if you could actually discern a Truth related to moving a mountain and exercise faith upon it, it would move. As we know, whatever we are "faithing" may or may not happen immediately but it will come into being in God's timing. Finally, there is a sobering fact in verse 6a of Hebrews 11: "and without faith it is impossible to please God…". There were Old Testament Jews who pleased God and some of them are mentioned by name in Hebrews 11, but (unlike us in Christ) according to the last verse in the chapter "… none of these were made perfect…". In other words, these were declared righteous (right with God) but not yet perfect. New Testament believers are both righteous and perfect only because of the Perfect One living within us. You may find it difficult to buy into this but I firmly believe that your name would appear in a New Covenant Hall of Faith, not because of anything you have thought, said, or done but because of the righteous and perfect One living within you. So we needn't feel puffed up because of what I have just proposed but we should all have a balanced sense of how God views us. https://www.gotquestions.org/how-does-God-see-me.html If you are like me you don't feel perfect or righteous but we can't and shouldn't argue with how God sees us. My failing, and perhaps yours, is that I do not always adequately exercise the faith available to me. So each of us must grow in that!!!!!

Ok, where can we find Truths upon which to exercise faith? You know the answer, 1) God's Word (the Bible) and 2) a Word from His Spirit. However we may run into problems with both of them. The Truths of the Bible are subject to whether they are open to us or others and interpretation. Truths from the Spirit are subject to our discernment. But, please do not be deterred from exercising faith out of fear (which is the opposite of faith). Discerning the meanings of promises in the Word are usually easier than words from the Spirit. We can check the meanings of Bible promises in Commentaries and from Bible teachers/preachers. Ascertaining whether or not it is the Spirit speaking to us comes from experience and trial and error. However, Jesus (Who is the Spirit – 2 Corinthians 3:17) says that we know His voice (John 10:27). In addition, we must be very careful with regard to circumstances and we should not buy into them without much prayer because they could be tests and/or false leadings from the world, the flesh and our enemy.

# MINOR CONTROVERSY

The following is not a raging disagreement, but one worth mentioning. Those on one side of the issue (perhaps the majority) believe that faith being spoken of in the Word is that same faith with which we are born and that we use it to become saved. The other side believes that saving faith and everyday faith it is a part of the gift received supernaturally at the point of salvation. But as a practical matter it does not really matter which side of the issue you buy into since if you are born again from above the faith that you posses and exercise is that same faith spoken of in Scripture. One sub-issue that <u>does</u> matter greatly, however, is the **source** of our day-to-day maturing in faith and God's Word says that "Faith comes from hearing and hearing from the Word of God." (Romans 10:17)

# GOD EXPECTS UNINTERRUPTED FAITH

Now allow me to expose you to a real shocker buried at the end of Romans 14:23c: "...whatever is not from faith is sin". What this obviously means is that any and every thought, word, and deed we engage in apart from faith receives the dreaded "s" designation. Do not listen to the weak-kneed apologists that say to us, "surely God does not mean this." If you believe as I do that God says what He means and means what He says you will take more seriously your connection to Him in our everyday life. So when you ask for forgiveness of sins this includes everything thought, said, and done apart from faith. The impression I receive is that God wants us to relate to Him in all things through Bible reading/study, listening for His voice, and continuously conversing with Him and seeking His direction and approval. (Proverbs 3:6) Of course we will fail in this most of the time but we cannot avoid the "s" judgment that is deserved at the end of most of our thoughts, words, and deeds.

We know from Jesus' life that He constantly both lived and walked by faith. 1 John 2:6 tells us that "the one who says he remains in Him (Jesus) ought, himself also, walk just as He walked." So just how did He walk? In His Father's presence, in Love, in Peace, i.e in every bit of the fruit of the Spirit (Galatians 5: 22-23). Our problem is that we just don't stay connected to God. And why is that?

Jesus is the Author and Finisher of our faith (Hebrews 12:2). As Author He is our Lord, our Captain, our Commander and as our Finisher He is our Sustainer and our Supporter. So He equips us and nourishes us. So we have His faith and cannot lose it. We will never receive additional faith but we can and should grow in it as we exercise it (like a muscle – a spiritual one). Again, while this is controversial, we see in Galatians 2:20 that it is usually translated "we live by faith **in** the Lord" when grammatically "in" is in the <u>genitive</u> case which is possessive and means the faith **of** Jesus. So, if it is Jesus' faith then it is perfect yet He permits us to use it. Being the Alpha and Omega of our faith is another way of saying that Jesus is both the Source as well of the Object of our faith which we may exercise with His permission.

# FAITH CONTROVERSY CAMPS

Ok, let us explore the two sides of the faith controversy, not for the purpose of taking sides but to understand where each is coming from. Remember that it has nothing to do with our exercise of faith because if you are born again, the faith that you have, as a believer, works every time you put it into play properly. We will use as our context Ephesians 2:8-9, "For by grace you have been saved through **faith**; and **this** is not of yourselves, it is the gift of God; not a result of works, so that no one may boast".

Next let us give each side of the controversy an identifying label:

1) the <u>Grammar Camp</u> which contends that since the word "**this**" [some translations use "that"] is neuter case and "**faith**" is feminine case they are not in case agreement which means that "this/that" does <u>not</u> refer to "faith." So from that contention this camp argues that faith is that with which a person is born. It further reasons that since a person is not born again until he/she has exercised this inborn faith, the faith being spoken of must be that which all men possess.

2) the <u>Context Camp</u> which counters by saying that since salvation is "**not of yourselves**" and inborn faith is "of yourselves" that the faith exercised could <u>not</u> be the inborn faith but must be one imparted instantaneously at the point of decision. There are a few verses that this camp might use to support its contention. One of those is John 6:47: "Truly, truly, I say to you, whoever believes has eternal life". As is usually the case, the verb "believes" is actually the verb "faith" in Koine Greek (**πιστεύων),** so this camp would contend that only believers have eternal life and since that is the case, the faith must be God given instead of inborn. What they see is that the verse does **not** say that the person believing/faithing **will** receive eternal life but that he/she **has** eternal life. To this camp this means that receiving saving faith and eternal life are bestowed simultaneously. Other supporting verses are found later in this paper.

But, of course, the Grammar Camp could rebut this by saying that the inborn faith secured the salvation for the believer as well as eternal life. Again, there is nothing to be gained in this debate and we believers are not to be contentious (1 Corinthians 11:16). In the final analysis it doesn't matter whether your faith was inborn or bestowed at the point of salvation as long as it connected you with Jesus who granted you salvation (2 Corinthians 5:17).

Both camps seem to have reasonable assertions but keep in mind that you do not have to take sides since your rebirth faith connects you to Truth and 2 Timothy 2:24 commands us: "And the Lord's servant must not be quarrelsome but must be kind to everyone, able to teach, not resentful".

Abraham who was not born again is known as the father of our faith (Romans 4:16). His example would seem to favor the Grammar Camp except for the fact that while being declared righteous he was not made perfect (Hebrews 11:40) and evidently did not receive eternal life at that time while the verse John 6:47 we looked at earlier states that "... whoever believes (faiths) has eternal life...". God accepted his human faith and credited it to him as righteousness but not eternal life. So, again, as we try to unravel all this we wind up "chasing our tail." [But we are not dogs!]

Ok, with our heads spinning, let us now and forevermore leave this potentially divisive debate to contentious eggheads and focus on learning more about properly exercising faith. After all, as was said before: the faith you and I have as believers is connected to God's power and works every time it is exercised. [Whew!!!!!]

Now, I know that you still have questions about what exactly is meant by faith but I do not know any quick fix for you. As we continue to discuss it based on Scripture I hope that eventually the light bulb will come on and you will be able to zero in on its exact meaning. [Mark 9:23b (Jesus speaking) "...Everything is possible for one who believes". i.e who "faiths" πιστεύοντι)]

# INADEQUACY OF THE ENGLISH LANGUAGE

I suspect that you have at times believed the Lord for something that did not come about. (we all have!) If it was based on one of His many promises you know that Jesus does not lie so it should point up the fact that the problem must be with you or an understanding of the concept of faith. Agreed? The word usually translated "believe" [πίστις is the root word] is in fact some form of the Koine Greek word "faith," but if in context when it is a verb, English does not have a verb form for faith and it sadly must be translated "believe." And, as was pointed out earlier, "believe" is a broader concept and, as you know full well, not all of our beliefs are true/factual/ legitimate/valid. Remember from our discussion of Hebrews 11:1 that faith is both <u>assurance</u> and <u>conviction</u>. So when we "faith" something there is an accompanying assurance of its reality and the faith itself is the evidence of its actuality. I hope that you are slowly realizing that our "beliefs" are a creation of our soul (mind/ will/ emotions) and that our "faith" must be based on Truth. And, remember, the only place we find Truth is with God: **Jesus Himself** (the Living Word) – John 14:6; **The Bible** (the written Word) – John 17:17; and **God's Spirit** (Both Jesus and the Father are the Spirit)– Galatians 4:6 and Romans 8:11; and by definition, the Holy Spirit is the Spirit. These Truths should not come as a surprise since according to Deuteronomy 6:4, God is One.

# EXPLORING TRUTH

Before we leave these thoughts let's explore the Truths that we encounter daily. The written Truth is for the most part pretty straight forward but, as we know, can easily be misunderstood or misinterpreted so we need to study the whole counsel of God and comprehend with care. The Bible is the best commentary on itself so exploring parallel verses/passages is a necessary undertaking. In addition, commentaries can be useful for additional perspectives. As we study, the leading of the Spirit will direct us into Truth (John 16:13) since that is one of His responsibilities. A word of caution, words from the Spirit apart from the written Word, can be rejected or overridden by our flesh so we need to carefully check ourselves to see if we are truly walking in the Spirit and confirm that what we are hearing is Jesus' voice and consistent with God's Word. And, to be sure, they cannot contradict each other. Are we open to whatever God supplies as a result to our faith prayer? And again, beware of coincidence since it may just play into our desire and/or even be a spiritual test. Have you discussed it with someone who has Godly knowledge and wisdom and who holds you accountable? Learn to recognize His voice and how He leads/speaks to you (John 10:27). Learn from each encounter with His Spirit while remembering that God works in mysterious ways (Isaiah 55:8-9). Never rely on feelings but wait for and expect a sense of absolute peace and not doubt and/or have anxiety. Remember that *feelings, emotions, and deep-seated affections are* of the flesh *and* can easily lead us astray. Never "put your hands on" the result. Examine your emotions and do not be lead by them. Beware if someone else tells you that God told him/her that you should do something. It might be genuine but if you are a mature believer, expect Him to speak to you directly or give you a leading. If you feel convicted by a Bible verse or passage/sermon/teaching/ etc., pay attention and respond. Unless you realize that you have special gifting, beware of dreams/visions, but do not ignore them completely because God does operate this way at times – if it is genuine you should have a STRONG "knowing." about its authenticity. Pray for closed doors in case it is based on your fleshly desire instead of Truth.

# FAITH: ADVENTURE ON THE RIGHTEOUS PATH

Ok, back to faith: faith makes it possible for us in the present to have a secure "knowing" spiritually about something that will come in its fullness either now or at some point in the future. And this "knowing" is, in a spiritual sense, solid "substance" and "evidence" (Hebrews 11:1). There is a promise in Psalm 32:8: "I will instruct you and teach you in the way which you should go; I will counsel you with My eye upon you". And, as we know, He will do this through His Word and through His Spirit. Our part is to get to know and obey both. As John Piper put it, "In other words, faith grasps – lays hold of – God's preciousness so firmly that in the faith itself there is the substance of the goodness and sweetness promised. Faith is spiritual apprehending or perceiving or tasting or sensing of God's promises as real. And this means that faith has the substance in that faith. Faith's enjoyment of the promise is a kind of substantial down payment of the coming of physical reality". (Wow, how poetic!)

You have, no doubt, heard the invitation to "name it and claim it." Obviously believers do not have a "blank check" to name just anything they might want but, as we have learned, what we "faith" will come about if it is based on something concrete promised by God. So there is nothing wrong with making a request of God but just don't call it faith. In this case it is a **petition**. [I have often wondered how many have bought into this "name it and claim it" invitation and fallen away and given up on God because their claim was not fulfilled.

Please allow me to ask you a personal question: When you were hearing the gospel, did you have a "knowing" that you were going to be saved? And then when you prayed the sinners' prayer did you "know" with your whole being that you were saved? Rest assured, that sense of "knowing" is from God, not your emotions. And has this "knowing" stayed with you? If you were saved as a child these may be hard questions for you but if you were saved after childhood these are perfectly reasonable questions. You cannot be saved again, however, if you ever have doubts it is a simple matter to talk openly to God and tell Him what you did earlier and then 1) confess to Him that you know that you sin (Romans 3;23), 2) that you want all of your sins (past, present, and future) to be forever forgiven (1 John 1:9), and 3) that You want Jesus to reign over you from now on (Galatians 4:6). No one should sit in church unsaved or doubt his/her salvation. There should be no embarrassment to making secure one's salvation. You meant to be saved, and perhaps you were, but if you are not sure, our enemy will have a field day with you. Once you have spiritual confirmation or reconfirmation of your salvation it would be wise to write down the date, time, and circumstance as your spiritual birthday and hold that up to our enemy when he attacks. "Faithing" is knowing and knowing is "faithing".

You can now say, "I am saved," "I am being saved," and "I will be saved" since while your salvation is sealed at the moment of rebirth it is a process that continues "until that day." (a mystery?) Between each point on that continuum is a faith bridge (from faith to faith (Romans 1;17) and that bridge is sure – take it to the bank! And the Truth tells us that God's gifts and calling are irrevocable (Romans 11:29).

# ON APPLYING YOUR FAITH

So, upon what will you apply your faith? How many promises would you think God makes available through His Word? I haven't counted them but reportedly there are 8,810 and 7,487 of them are made by God to men. Some of these you and I can claim and some we cannot. Just for practice take a couple of promises right now and confidently claim them by faith without doubting:

> **Matthew 11:28** "Come to Me, all who are weary and heavy -laden, and I will give you rest".

> **Isaiah 41:10** "Do not fear, for I am with you, Do not anxiously look about you, for I am your God, I will strengthen you, surely I will help you, Surely I will uphold you with My righteous right hand".

Simply pray these and others back to God and make your requests known to Him. If you are right with Him at the moment He has freely obligated Himself to make them happen. I challenge you too identify such promises as you read through the Bible or you can even look at Amazon

Books for Bible promise books, some as inexpensive as $1.95 or used for as little as 25¢. I take 11 travel-promise-cards with me to claim along the way and they are very reassuring and calming. Searching out God's promises that are open to us gets us into His Word, draws us even closer to Him, and allows us to know Him better. This is not self serving but satisfies His command in 2 Timothy 2:15 and transforms us into worthy workmen.

Rest assured that God will allow each of us to undergo tests of various types during our lives in Christ and every one will be tests of our faith to one degree or another. While tests are not always pleasant they serve God's purpose as with these He matures us and continually conforms us to the image of His Son. 1 Peter 1:6b-7 "...you have been distressed by various trials, so that the proof of your faith, being more precious than gold which perishes though tested/refined by fire, may be found to result in praise, glory and honor at the revelation of Jesus Christ".

As we walk in faith we are not alone in the journey since Christ our Lord walks with us. As we see this world degenerating before our eyes, 1 John 5:4 tells us that "For whoever has been born of God overcomes the world; and this is the victory that has overcome the world: our faith". By faith we have overcome the perverse world system that is sold out to sin and seeks to trap us with its many temptations. And in 2 Corinthians 10:4 "the weapons of our warfare are not of the flesh, but divinely powerful for the destruction of fortresses". One of God's many names is Jehovah Jireh (God will provide). He is our Provider and faith is a spiritual bank card for God's Teller machine (GTM) where He has stocked your and my accounts with an inexhaustible endowment of perfect answers to our prayers of faith. We may make as many withdrawals as we desire but what we fail to withdraw disappears forever.

Now for some additional insight: Allow me to give you examples of some types of prayer to help you better grasp the Biblical concept of prayer and add to your concept of faith.

https://www.orbcfamily.org/blog/prayer/7-different-types-of-pra/yer-in-the-bible

√   Prayer of Faith: "Lord, I had a sinful thought about my neighbor and ask you to forgive me of it, cleanse me of it, and keep me from it". [based on **1 John 1:9** "*If we confess our sins He is faithful and righteous to forgive us our sins and cleanse us from all unrighteousness.*"]

God has committed Himself to honor this prayer because of His Word.

√   Prayer of Petition: "Lord, our family needs direction regarding this job opportunity in another state. Make clear to us your will".

We must be "prayed up" and take our hands off of the opportunity, freeing God to reveal and deliver His will.

√ Prayer if <u>Intercession</u>: "Lord, I see a need of funding for a mission to rebuild a church building in Ukraine and I ask you to provide for this through our church body and the community".

[**1 Timothy 2:2** "First of all, then, I urge that requests, prayers, intercession, and thanksgiving be made in behalf of all people,]

If we have no confessed sin, God may honor the request but has not obligated Himself to do so. He may honor this kind of prayer in one instance but not in another for reasons known only to Him.

√ Prayer of <u>Thanksgiving</u>: "Lord we bow before you and thank you for your daily provision for us and we thank you especially for this food and ask you to bless it for our use".

[**Exodus 23:25a** "You shall serve the Lord your God, and He will bless your bread and your water...".]

Again, we must be free of unconfessed sin, and since this appears to be a sub-type of the Prayer of Faith you can expect it to be honored.

√ Prayer of <u>Worship</u>: "Worthy are you, our Lord and God, to receive glory and honor and power, for you created all things, and by your will, they existed and were created". **Revelation 4:11**

As always we must come before the throne of grace as pure as Jesus after we have asked forgiveness for our sins and to be filled with (controlled by) His Spirit.

√   Corporate Prayer: "Heavenly Father, we gather as a church to ask You to make fruitful and protect these brothers as they go out today to share the gospel with inmates in the local State prison".

[**Matthew 18:20** "For where two or three have gathered together in My name, I am there in their midst."]

There must not be any unconfessed sin among those in the prayer circle in order to have a direct channel to the Lord who will intercede for the group.

√   Prayer of Consecration: "Father, I present my body to Your Son Jesus as a living sacrifice and I present the members of my body to Him as instruments of righteousness. And since my body has been bought with His blood it rightfully belongs to Him. I acknowledge that it is a temple of Your Holy Spirit, use me for Your glory I pray."

[**Joshua 3:5** "Then Joshua said to the people, "Consecrate yourselves, for tomorrow the Lord will do wonders among you".]

Obviously consecration would begin with confession and then a setting apart of oneself (or 2 or more) for the task ahead.

√ Prayer of the <u>Holy Spirit</u>: "Lord, I do not know how to pray about this situation but I trust Your Spirit to know the proper words.

> [**Romans 8:26-27** "In the same way, the Spirit helps us in our weakness. We do not know what we ought to pray for, but the Spirit Himself intercedes for us through wordless groans. And He who searches our hearts knows the mind of the Spirit because the Spirit intercedes for God's people in accordance with the will of God".]

Needless to say, our relinquishing to the One who knows how to appropriately pray will be honored by the Lord for the believer who is at that moment right with Him.

**Faith Gems** From Manley Beasley, <u>Adventures in Faith</u>, Foundational Truth Publications, May 1979. [Went to be with the Lord in 2018 at age 58]

√ Faith is God/Truth dependency, as self dependency ends
√ Faith calms in the midst of the storm
√ Faith is confidence
√ Faith treats the future as here and now
√ Faith treats the seemingly impossible as possible
√ Faith is <u>of</u> Jesus not in or on Him (i.e. genitive case)
√ Faith is the opposite of fear
√ Jesus is both the object and source of the believer's faith

√ Jesus taught by example and continues to teach us to live by faith

√ Performing the works of God require "faithing" His Son, Jesus

√ Components of faith include the intellect, emotion, and volition

√ Faith is a spirit world faculty operating in the physical world

√ Faith is victory, not striving (1John 5:4)

√ Faith holds our old man in the position of death. . . . . [reckon it so!]

√ Not acting in faith is sin

√ Faith involves 2 steps: 1) Claiming a promise/Word, 2: Believing it **is** honored

√ God does not begin with a need but with the supply for that need

√ Faith is not safe but reckless

√ Faith is not faith unless tested

√ Faith rebels against our human nature

√ Faith subscribes to the theology of victory

√ 90% of us play it safe so that we do not have to walk by faith

√ Enemies of faith: doubt, human hope, reason, feelings, sacrifice, ignorance, dead works, bargaining, sympathy, insincere confession

√ An invitation from the Lord allowed Peter to walk on water by faith-gift

**John Wesley** proclaimed that our enemy gives the church a substitute for faith: mental assent

[And if you make yourself believe something, that my friend is simply "make believe."]

Three summary points from **Warren Wiersby** (went to be with the Lord in 2019):

- Faith has a beginning point: hearing the Word of God (Romans 10:17)
- Faith grows out of a relationship with God, (trusting Him in all things)
- Faith motivates us to do the will of God. (ex. Abraham offering Isaac)
- Faith in action gives us a testimony.

This paper is my legacy (defined as *something of value bequeathed to another or others.)* And what could be of more value than becoming right with God through faith, applying and growing in faith, and being destined to spend eternity with Him after one's physical death? Faith has always been the key to pleasing Him in an intimate relationship and in the latter days it was extended to non Jews (we Gentiles) following the Life, death, burial, resurrection, and ascension of God's only begotten Son, Jesus Christ.

# SIGNIFICANT FAITH VERSES THROUGHOUT THE BIBLE

Oftentimes when we read a Bible verse or hear a sermon/ teaching point we think of a verse(s) that may seem to contradict, and that causes conflict in our minds and perhaps suspicion or mistrust. The following verse commentaries (Italics) are explanations aimed at easing some of the conflicts. Find the verse you think contradicts and read the commentary.

# OLD TESTAMENT

- "Faith" (Strong's 529, 530) appears 2 times in the **OT**:
- "faithful" (Strong's 539, 571, 539, 529, 530, 540) appears 28 times.
- "faithfully" (Strong's 530, 571) appears 7 times in the **OT**.
- "faithfulness" (Strong's 530) appears around 20 times in the **OT**

▲ Numbers 12:7 "*It is* not this way *for* My servant **Moses**; He is faithful in all My household;"

> God wants us to faith walk with Him, not walk as the world does.

▲ 1 Samuel 2:35 "But I will raise up for Myself a **faithful priest** who will do according to what is in My heart and My soul; and I will build him an enduring house, and He will walk before My anointed always."

> And we, as God's anointed priests, are to live by faith.

▲ 1Samuel 26:23 "And the Lord will repay each man *for* his righteousness and his **faithfulness**; for the Lord handed you (Saul) over to me (David) today, but I refused to reach out with my hand against the Lord's anointed (King Saul)".

> Living by faith is a moment by moment lifestyle.

▲ Nehemiah 9:8 "You found his heart **(Abram) faithful** before You, And made a covenant with him to give *him* the land of the Canaanite, of the Hittite and the Amorite, of the Perizzite, the Jebusite, and the Girgashite—To give *it* to his(Abram's) descendants. And You have fulfilled Your promise, Because You are righteous."

> Faithful living has its rewards in this life and for your descendants.

▲ Psalm 31:23 "Love the LORD, all His godly ones! The LORD watches over the **faithful** but fully repays the one who acts arrogantly."

> God's watchcare is a valuable reward for faithfulness.

▲ Psalm 101:6 "My eyes shall be upon the **faithful** of the land, that they may dwell with me; One who walks in a blameless way is one who will serve me."

> God watches over the faithful and allows them to serve Him.

▲ Proverbs 13:17 "A wicked messenger falls into adversity, But a **faithful** messenger *brings* healing."

> Faith yields healing outcomes.

▲ Proverbs 25:13 "Like the cold of snow in the time of harvest Is a **faithful** messenger to those who send him, For he refreshes the soul of his masters."

> Walking faithfully pleases the masters and the Master.

▲ Proverbs 27:6 "**Faithful** are the wounds of a friend, But deceitful are the kisses of an enemy."

> It takes great faith to compassionately chastise a friend.

▲ Proverbs 28:20 "A **faithful** person will abound with blessings, But one who hurries to be rich will not go unpunished."

> The faithful believer seeks eternal riches.

▲ Isaiah 8:2 "And I will take to Myself **faithful witnesses** for testimony, **Uriah** the priest and **Zechariah** the son of Jeberechiah."

> *Faithful believers will be consecrated for service.*

▲ Habakkuk 2:4 "Behold, his soul is puffed up; it is not upright within him, but the **righteous** shall live by his faith."

> *The faith walk is a 24/7 endeavor.*

# NEW TESTAMENT

- "Faith" appears around 250 times in **NT**, "faithful" around 155 times, "faithfully" 1time, and "faithless" 4 times

- In the **NT**  "faith" = Strong's 1680, 3640, 4102,
        "faithful" = Strong's 4103
        "faithfully" = Strong's 4103
        "faithfulness" = Strong's none
        "faithless" = Strong's 571

▲ Matthew 6:30 "But if God so clothes the grass of the field, which is alive today and tomorrow is thrown into the furnace, will He not much more clothe you? You of little faith."

> Here little faith is not an issue of the quantity of faith but of lacking confidence in God (I.e not expecting God's Truth to prevail).

▲ Matthew 8:10 "Now when Jesus heard this, He marveled and said to those who were following, "Truly I say to you, I have not found such great faith with anyone in Israel."

> While the term "τοσαύτην" (so great) usually <u>does</u> mean quantity it can also be thought of as the opposite of "little" in Matthew 6:30. In both instances those believers referred to <u>have</u> that same faith but one exercises it wholeheartedly, fully expecting the result to happen whereas the others halfheartedly. Neither party needs or will receive more faith in the sense of quantity since it is a God-given single-unit capability/ bestowal. Keep in mind that a mountain can be moved when this power is based on a promise/command from God and exercised wholeheartedly; and this is not a matter of human commitment but a spiritual "knowing" and trust that this is the will of God. If "great" in this verse means quantity then it would be in contradiction of the mustard seed response by Jesus to His disciples in Matthew 13:32.

▲ Matthew 8:26 "He said to them, "Why are you afraid, you men of little faith?" Then He got up and rebuked the winds and the sea, and it became perfectly calm."

> All believers <u>have</u> faith so it is not a matter of the degree or quantity of that faith but

of their failure to apply it at that moment. Faith is a faculty but it is also a moment-by-moment choice. At that moment on the water the disciples unanimously chose fear over faith. If we are with Jesus then we know Truth and the Truth will always prevail.

▲ Matthew 9:2 "And they brought to Him a paralytic lying on a bed. Seeing their faith, Jesus said to the paralytic, 'Take courage, son; your sins are forgiven."

In effect, with His command, He saw that the man and his friends would believe and trust Him, take the courage that He was offering, and healing would be the result through their faith.

▲ Matthew 9:22 "But Jesus turning and seeing her said, "Daughter, take courage; your faith has made you well." At once the woman was made well."

It should go without saying that Jesus healed the woman through her faith and her faith was not the source of her healing. Faith as a relational faculty has no power in itself but it connected the woman to the power of Jesus, Who seeing this healed the woman.

▲ Matthew 9:29 "Then He touched their eyes, saying, "It shall be done to you according to your faith."

See previous commentary.

▲ Matthew 14:31 "Immediately Jesus stretched out His hand and took hold of him, and said to him (Peter), "You of little faith, why did you doubt?"

> As stated previously, this is not a question of the quantity of faith but of a tentative or halfhearted exercise of it.

▲ Matthew 15:28 "Then Jesus said to her, "O woman, your faith is great; it shall be done for you as you wish." And her daughter was healed at once".

> This woman was exercising faith wholeheartedly so that Jesus could and would heal he daughter. He saw her faith and granted her request

▲ Matthew 16:8 "But Jesus, aware of this, said, 'You men of little faith, why are you discussing among yourselves the fact that you have no bread'?"

> See Matthew 14:31 commentary.

▲ Matthew 17:20 "And He said to them,'Because of the littleness of your faith; for truly I say to you, if you have faith the size of a mustard seed, you will say to this mountain, 'Move from here to there,' and it will move; and nothing will be impossible to you."

> [See previous commentary.] Jesus explains clearly that faith, exercised properly, will

always succeed in bringing about even the most incredible results. But, of course, it must be based on Truth from the Word and/or the Spirit.

▲ Matthew 21:21 "And Jesus answered and said to them, "Truly I say to you, if you have faith and do not doubt, you will not only do what was done to the fig tree (made barren), but even if you say to this mountain, 'Be taken up and cast into the sea,' it will happen."

Here Jesus reiterates that faith must be exercised wholeheartedly and He implies with the mountain example that it will bring about even unimaginable results.

▲ Matthew 23:23 "Woe to you, scribes and Pharisees, hypocrites! For you tithe mint and dill and cumin, and have neglected the weightier provisions of the law: justice and mercy and faith; but these are the things you should have done without neglecting the others."

From the beginning faith has trumped completely works alone and that faith will facilitate the obedience expected by God. Correct order: faith first and obedience will follow.

▲ Mark 2:5 "And Jesus seeing <u>their</u> faith (those who brought the paralytic to Jesus) said to the paralytic, 'son, your sins are forgiven'."

> Jesus reveals in the "a" part of the verse that even the faith of others can bring about a result in another.

▲ Mark 5:34 "And He said to her, 'Daughter, your faith has made you well; go in peace and be healed of your affliction'."

> See Matthew 9:22 commentary

▲ Mk 10:52 "And Jesus said to him, 'Go; your faith has made you well. Immediately he regained his sight and began following Him on the road'."

> See Matthew 9:22 commentary

▲ Luke 7:9 "Now when Jesus heard this, He marveled at him, and turned and said to the crowd that was following Him, 'I say to you, not even in Israel have I found such great faith'."

> Again, this is not a question of quantity or degree of faith but of the proper exercise of it, which in this case was wholehearted.

▲  Luke 12:28 "But if God so clothes the grass in the field, which is alive today and tomorrow is thrown into the furnace, how much more will He clothe you? You men of little faith"!

> See Matthew 14:31 commentary

▲  Luke 17:5 "The apostles said to the Lord, 'Increase our faith'!"

> The apostles did not "get it," they saw faith as a variable quantity rather than a set comprehensive relational faculty available to all believers.

▲  Luke 17:6 "And the Lord said, 'If you had faith like a mustard seed, you would say to this mulberry tree, Be uprooted and be planted in the sea and it would obey you'."

> See Matthew 21:21 commentary

▲  Luke 17:19 "And He said to him, 'Stand up and go; your faith has made you well'."

> See Matthew 9:22 commentary

***Faith is not mentioned in the gospel of John (even the one whom Jesus loved) (John 13:23(?)

▲ Acts 3:16 "And on the basis of <u>faith</u> in His name, it is the name of Jesus which has strengthened this man whom you see and know; and the <u>faith</u> w**hich comes through Him** has given him this perfect health in the presence of you all."

Ok, let's begin to unpack this thorny verse by stating categorically that while it may appear on the surface that Jesus' name can be used as an incantation (magic word) that is absolutely <u>not</u> the case except if God wills and allows it.)

Remember that in Mark 16:17-18 Jesus had instructed that His disciples should perform miracles in His name and they were simply obeying this direct command. Next think about how you and I pray. We also obediently say somewhere in our prayers "in Jesus name". This is in response to multiple promises/commands: John 14: 13-14, 15:16, 16:23-26, etc. In addition, we know that the faith of any and all believers comes from and through Him. There is no explicit indication here that the healed man even had faith but we know for sure that the paralytic's friends and Jesus' disciples did, being thoroughly persuaded through His Spirit that He could and would heal the man. So the man was healed in the name of Jesus not by it. So Peter obediently offered his faith prayer in the name of Jesus in the full knowledge of whatever he asked in Jesus name his Lord would do so that the Father would be glorified in the Son. And this saying found its way into John's gospel 14:13-14. So in humility Peter was not taking any credit for either the faith or the healing of the man. Jesus did it all!

▲ Acts 14:9 "This man was listening to Paul as he spoke, who, when he had fixed his gaze on him and had seen that he had faith to be made well.'

The faith of the man was given to him by the Spirit of Jesus in order that Paul could see through his spiritual eyes that the man believed that Jesus could and would make him well. Spiritual insight such as Paul's is a gift bestowed upon those whom God chooses to use in particular ways.

▲ Acts 14: 27 "When they had arrived and gathered the church together, they began to report all things that God had done with them and how He had opened a door of faith to the Gentiles."

It seems to be clear from this verse that the acquisition of faith must be allowed by God, which is also indicated in Acts 16:14 with Lydia.

▲ Acts 16:5 "So the churches were being strengthened in the faith, and were increasing in number daily."

> Faith does not increase but can be strengthened by reading/studying the Word, through the Holy Spirit, through teaching, exercising it, and through fellowship with others of faith.

▲ Acts 26:18 "...to open their eyes so that they may turn from darkness to light and from the dominion of Satan to God, that they may receive forgiveness of sins and an inheritance among those who have been sanctified **by faith** in Me."

> "Faithing" Jesus to rule our lives brings salvation to be sure, but much, much more as we walk with Him in that faith we are being set aside for greater service. And this verse is only the "tip of the iceberg". (Ephesians 3:20)

▲ Romans 1:17 "For in it (*the gospel*) the righteousness of God is revealed from faith to faith as it is written, But the righteous *man* shall live by faith."

> Since there appears to be no clear meaning from either context or Koine Greek we can take comfort in agreeing that the prepositions "from (or out from)" (ek) and "to (or into)" (eis) have a clear meaning of faith moving from one position to another. From there it becomes a matter of interpretation and I

would suggest that Paul may have had in mind multiple applications:

√ OT faith by which none were made perfect vs NT faith
√ A believer sharing the gospel with a ready prospect
√ Influence of one believer's faith upon another
√ Progressive growth in one's exercise of faith
√ From start to finishing of ones faith (Hebrews 12:2)

▲ Romans 3:28 "For we maintain that a man is justified by faith apart from works of the Law."

This verse makes it crystal clear that the Law cannot bring justification. (I.e. justification being a change in a person's condition from a state of sin to that of righteousness)

▲ Romans 3:30 "...since indeed God who will justify the circumcised by **faith** and the uncircumcised through **faith** is one." [i.e Jew vs. Gentile]

Again, repetition of the Truth that faith is open to "whosoever will."

▲ Romans 3:31 "Do we then nullify the Law through faith? May it never be! On the contrary, we establish the Law."

> God's Law is immutable and only faith allows the believer to obey it.

▲ Rom 4:5 "But to the one who does not work, but believes in Him who justifies the ungodly, his faith is credited as righteousness."

> A person of faith is righteous, which cannot be earned.

▲ Romans 4:9 "Is this blessing then on the circumcised, or on the uncircumcised also? For we say, 'FAITH WAS CREDITED TO ABRAHAM AS RIGHTEOUSNESS'."

> The blessings of God under the New Covenant have been extended through faith beyond His original chosen people, Israel.

▲ Romans 4:11 ",,,and he received the sign of circumcision, a seal of the righteousness of the faith which he had while uncircumcised, so that he might be the father of all who believe without being circumcised, that righteousness might be credited to them,"

> This verse shows clearly that Abram's faith and the resulting righteousness preceded the seal/sign of circumcision which is a mirror of NT faith and righteousness which precedes water baptism

▲ Rom 4:12 "...and the father of circumcision (Abraham)
to those who not only are of the circumcision, but
who also follow in the steps of the faith of our father
Abraham which he had while uncircumcised."

> Abraham is the recognized father of all who
> came after him in "faithing" God, whether Jew
> or Gentile. The former being identified by the
> seal/sign of circumcision and the Gentiles by
> water baptism.

▲ Romans 4:13 "For the promise to Abraham or to his
descendants that he would be heir of the world was
not through the Law, but through the righteousness
of faith."

> The intention is not to imply that faith itself
> is righteous but the practice of it is rewarded
> by God with righteousness.

▲ Rom 4:20 "...yet, with respect to the promise of God, he
did not waver in unbelief but grew strong in faith,
giving glory to God,"

> Notice that Abraham's faith was not increased
> but as he applied it in more and more situations
> he was more effective for God's purposes.

▲ Romans 5:1 "Therefore, having been justified by faith, we have peace with God through our Lord Jesus Christ",

> When a person initially "faiths" the Lord he/she becomes a believer, is made right with God and is assured of a place with Him in heaven.

▲ Romans 5:2 "...through whom also we have obtained our introduction by faith into this grace in which we stand; and we exult in hope of the glory of God."

> Eternal life means being right with God and destined to spend eternity with Him. Yes, Jesus did die for the sins of everyone in the world and this eternal life is a gift offered by God but it is not automatic but like any transaction must be accepted and in this case by responding to the gospel (good news). The gift is in Christ Jesus (Romans 6:23) which means that a person must go to Him. (think prayer) John. 14:6 tells us that in reality Jesus is the Life itself. The same verse explains that one must go through Jesus to be introduced by faith into God's spiritual grace through which eternal life is conveyed.

▲ Romans 9:30 "What shall we say then? That Gentiles, who did not pursue righteous-ness, attained righteousness, even the righteousness which is by faith";

> Gentiles, rather than seeking righteousness through the Law or by good deeds, seek to know Jesus and be right with God through Him. This is just like Abram and other Old Testament saints who sought the Lord, obeyed Him, and were awarded righteousness.

▲ Romans 9:32 "Why? Because they did not pursue it by faith, but as though it were by works. They stumbled over the stumbling stone",

> This verse is another proof that salvation/ eternal life cannot be attained in any other way than through faith. Jesus is the stumbling stone over which all who reject Him or try to go around Him stumble not realizing that He is the Way, the Truth, and the Life. (John 14:6)

▲ Romans10:8 "But what does it say? 'THE WORD IS NEAR YOU, IN YOUR MOUTH AND IN YOUR HEART' — that is, the word of faith which we are preaching',"[Good discussion verse]

> The path to being right with God and spending eternity with Him (faith) is found in His Word. The confession of this is designed to be expressed orally. (Romans 10:9)

▲ Romans 10:17 "So faith comes from hearing, and hearing by the Word of Christ."

> The source of faith is God and He has embedded it in His Word, the Bible. The ear is the usual gate through which the gospel message is received, although some obtain it through the eye gate.

▲ Romans 12:3 "For through the grace given to me I say to everyone <u>among</u> <u>you</u> not to think more highly of himself than he ought to think; but to think so as to have sound judgment, as God has allotted to each a measure of faith."

> Even though this is addressed to believers it should <u>not</u> necessarily be taken as an an endorsement of faith being allotted at rebirth since it is not perfectly clear exactly when the faith was allotted and there are scant verses to support the timing of its allotment either way.

▲ Romans 12:6 "Since we have gifts that differ according to the grace given to us, each of us is to exercise them accordingly: if prophecy, according to the proportion of his faith;"

[This is yet another thorny verse and requires a much more lengthy examination.]

> Our late pastor very often repeated the following crucial guideline for Bible study

and for "rightly dividing the Word" (2 Timothy 2:18): Context! Context! Context! With this in mind it is essential to point out that this verse is in the passage context of spiritual gifts. Paul rightly points out in verse 3 that all believers are "allotted a <u>measure</u> of faith" but in verse 6 he begins to talk about spiritual gifts, which are special endowments "...*for the equipping of the saints for the work of service, to the building up of the body of Christ"* And these <u>unique</u> gifts are granted to but a few. In this context, faith is so mentioned alongside prophecy since it is one of the **9 – 22** such gifts (depending who is doing the counting). So it would seem reasonable to conclude that the spiritual gift of faith would accompany this gift of prophecy. In Clarke's commentary we find that *"prophecy, in the New Testament, often means the gift of exhorting, preaching, or of expounding the Scriptures"* instead of "foretelling." And apparently the potency of the prophecy depends upon the "proportion" of the faith-gift possessed by the one expounding the Word. Proportion is defined as "a part, share, or number considered in comparative relation to a whole." So whereas "general faith" is a set quantity, the gift of faith appears to exist in varying proportions. (Yet another good discussion topic)

**Review**: So, thus far we have seen that there exist:

- √ The faith (a belief system stemming from the life and teachings, of Jesus of Nazareth (the Christ/Messiah) i.e the Christian faith as opposed to other faiths
- √ Faith, a faculty that Christian believers exercise for putting their confidence in Jesus and His Truths
- √ The spiritual gift of faith/faithfulness

▲ Romans 14:1 "Now accept the one who is weak in faith, but not for the purpose of passing judgment on his opinions."

> "Weak in faith" simply means that the "one" has not matured very much spiritually and is still trusting in "the elemental principles of the world" (Galatians 4:3) and not in Jesus. He/she is hesitant in stepping out in faith with God's truths/promises.

▲ Romans 14:22 "The faith which you have, have as your own conviction before God. Happy is he who does not condemn himself in what he approves." [Good discussion verse]

> We are still in the context of those with weak faith and those with strong faith. In this second verse of the context Paul is addressing mature believers who have stronger faith.

These allowed themselves to enjoy behaviors which were 1) hitherto condemned by the Law and 2) which may even have violated their principles when in spiritual infancy, childhood, and youth. He is admonishing them not to back away from their rightful freedom(s) in Christ. (i.e. to be confident in their mature faith) But as seen elsewhere not if it causes another to fall.

▲ Romans 14:23 "But he who doubts is condemned if he eats, because his eating is not from **faith;** and **whatever is not from faith is sin."** [Also a good discussion verse]

Still in the context of believers of weaker vs. stronger faith, Paul is saying that as one grows through the spiritual levels (infant, child, youth, mature, his/her knowledge and faith at each level will dictate appropriate behaviors.

▲ Romans 16:26 "...but now is manifested (*the gospel*), and by the Scriptures of the prophets, according to the commandment of the eternal God, has been made known to all the nations, leading to **obedience of faith."**

Since in the context the gospel is the subject, faith refereed to appears to be that of saving faith.

▲ 1Corinthians 2:5 "...so that your faith would not rest on the wisdom of men, but on the power of God."

> However flawed the presentation of the person sharing the gospel or any preaching, the impact of the message upon the hearer is from God's power. (i.e. we hear whatever God wants us to hear)

▲ 1Corinthians 12:9 "...to another faith by the same Spirit, and to another gifts of healing by the one Spirit."

> This is another verse concerning spiritual gifts and the special gift of faith/faithfulness.

▲ 2Corinthians 5:7 "...for we walk by faith, not by sight— ."

> Our Christian walk with Christ should be one of using our spiritual eyes and not our physical eyes as we live each moment by faith.

▲ 2Corinthians 10:15 "...not boasting beyond our measure, that is, in other men's labors, but with the hope that as your faith grows, we will be, within our sphere, enlarged even more by you."

> As discussed earlier, the quantity of faith is not an issue since faith the size of a mustard seed can move a mountain (Matthew 17:20), but how we mature in faith by exercising it in more situations.

▲ Galatians 2:16 "...nevertheless knowing that a man is not justified by the works of the Law but **through faith** in Christ Jesus, even we have believed in Christ Jesus, so that we may be **justified by faith** in Christ and not by the works of the Law; since by the works of the Law no flesh will be justified."

> An old definition of "justified" is just-as-if-I'd never sinned. In other words, all sins being forgiven makes one right with God and destined to spend eternity with Him. And it is that saving faith that prompts God to make it so. (i.e. one is not saved by faith but through it.)

▲ Galatians 2:20 "I have been crucified with Christ; and it is no longer I who live, but Christ lives in me; and the life which I now live in the flesh I live by faith in the Son of God, who loved me and gave Himself up for me."

> Again, walking with Christ is thinking, speaking, and behaving by what one sees with his/her spiritual eyes and not one's physical eyes.

▲ Galatians 3:2 "This is the only thing I want to find out from you: did you receive the Spirit by the works of the Law, or by hearing with faith?"

> When one receives the Spirit of Jesus (Galatians 4:6) it is not because of anything

done to try to please God but by the power of God and His Word as one "faiths" it. (Galatians 2:20)

▲ Galatians 3:8 "The Scripture, foreseeing that God would justify the Gentiles by faith, preached the gospel beforehand to Abraham, saying, "ALL THE NATIONS WILL BE BLESSED IN YOU."

Very interesting verse since it is not recorded in so many words in Genesis that God preached the gospel to Abraham but seemingly implied by the concluding quote in the verse.

▲ Galatians 3:9 "So then those who are of faith are blessed with Abraham, the believer."

Abraham believed (i.e. "faithed") God and it was reckoned to him as righteousness which made him right with God and destined him to spend eternity with Him; as are we. (Genesis 5:6, Romans 4:22)

▲ Galatians 3:11 "Now that no one is justified by the Law before God is evident; for, 'THE RIGHTEOUS MAN SHALL LIVE BY FAITH'."

Living by faith is the same as walking with Christ as described in the commentary of Galatians 2:20: thinking, speaking, and behaving by what one sees with his/her spiritual eyes and not one's physical eyes.

▲ Galatians 3:14 "...in order that in Christ Jesus the blessing of Abraham might come to the Gentiles, so that we would receive the promise of the Spirit through faith."

> Listen carefully! Justification is a one-time bestowal and is only part of salvation. Salvation involves a process of which justification is only one part. The Salvation of a person begins in eternity before the foundation of the world and ends in glorification as the saints of God dwell with Him forevermore. You have heard it said: "I am saved, I am being saved, and I will be saved. Therein lies the process and it is guaranteed and irrevocable from start to finish. (Romans 11:29) Get it?

▲ Galatians 3:22 "But the Scripture has shut up everyone under sin, so that the promise by faith in Jesus Christ might be given to those who believe."

> Man's sin took him out of the mode of innocence and caused his estrangement from God. God then allowed faith to be the only way back to fellowship with Himself.

▲ Galatians 3:23 "But before **faith** came, we were kept in custody under the Law, being confined for the **faith** that was destined to be revealed." [*But Abram was before the Law!*]

> Faith actually preceded the Law and dated back to Abram/Abraham but in NT times the Judiaizers had come from Israel to the Galatian church to try to convince the believers there that justification/salvation also demanded adherence to the Law. As you know, Paul preached against this and insisted that salvation is by God's grace through faith apart from the Law.

▲ Galatians 3:24 "Therefore the Law has become our tutor to lead us to Christ, so that we may be **justified by faith.**"

> The "us" in the verse applies solely to the Jew since the Law was never imposed upon us Gentiles. The "lead" in the verse means that the Jews' inability to obey the Law would compel them to seek the only viable way (faith).

▲ Galatians 3:26 "For you are all sons of God through faith in Christ Jesus."

> Paul is addressing the believers in the Galatian church. And that "faith" is an unshakable faith and not simply believing that He existed and was God's Son (as I believed for the first 32 years of my life).

▲ Galatians5:5 "For we through the Spirit, by faith, are waiting for the hope of righteousness."

> Biblical hope is a sure thing based on the Truth (from both the Word and the Holy Spirit). And the hope spoken of in this verse is the final stage of our salvation. (See commentary for Galatians. 3:14)

▲ Galatians 5:22 "But the fruit of the Spirit is love, joy, peace, patience, kindness, goodness, faithfulness."

> This is not a list of nine separate fruits, but nine characteristics of the (single) fruit of the Spirit. These describe what should be flowing from believers' lives as they allow the Holy Spirit to lead them.

▲ Ephesians 2:8 "For by grace you have been saved through faith; and that not of yourselves, it is the gift of God."

> As Americans our value system dictates that we earn whatever we receive, but that is not the acceptable path with regard to a relationship with God. He insists on faith as the path and His grace being His reciprocal response. [Grace being defined as unmerited favor]

▲ Ephesians 3:12 "in whom we have boldness and confident access through faith in Him."

> Unshakable faith in Jesus gives the believer unobstructed access to the Trinity as we are free from sin and filled with (controlled by the Holy Spirit.

▲ Ephesians 3:17 "...so that Christ may dwell in your hearts through faith; and that you, being rooted and grounded in love."

> This verse is a portion of Paul's prayer that the Ephesian believers might be strengthened with power through God's Spirit in the inner man. While the wording could be construed to mean that Christ might indwell them, keep in mind that no one can be <u>reborn</u> again so he seems to be encouraging them to use faith to be drawn into a deeper relationship with and knowledge of their Lord and Savior. [Something we all need]

▲ Ephesians 4:5 "...one Lord, one faith, one baptism."

> 1 Corinthians 12:3 tells us that no one can say Jesus is Lord (from the sincerity of his/her heart) except by the Holy Spirit. Through faith in Him we are united with His grace and become members of His family/kingdom. Baptism by the Spirit brings one

into spiritual union with Christ and unites believers as one body (1 Corinthians 12:13). Public water baptism is an outward sign of our spiritual conversion just as circumcision is an outward sign of being a Jew.

▲ Ephesians 6:16 "... in addition to all, taking up the shield of faith with which you will be able to extinguish all the flaming arrows of the evil one."

The shield of faith is the 4th piece of armor with which a child of God is equipped and is designed to allow him/her to extinguish the attack arrows of the evil one.

▲ Ephesians 6:23 "Peace be to the brethren, and love with faith, **from God** the Father **and** the Lord **Jesus** Christ."

Peace and love accompanied by faith are being evoked upon the Ephesian believers directly from the Trinity of God Himself through Paul's prayer. And by extension through faith we are able to worship in Spirit and Truth. (John 4:24) In addition we are enabled to carry out any and all God-directed works of service prepared for us. In addition this same faith allows us to engage effectively in spiritual warfare with the enemy.

▲ Philippians 1:25 "Convinced of this, I know that I will remain and continue with you all for your progress and joy in the faith."

> Our walk of faith is progressive in that as we exercise it in more and different situations we will become more and more effective faith warriors.

▲ Colossians 2:5 "For even though I am absent in body, nevertheless I am with you in spirit, rejoicing to see your good discipline and the **stability of your faith** in Christ." [faith should grow to a stable state] James 1:6

> Paul is a man of prayer and expresses a close spiritual connection with the Colossian church even though not with them physically at the time of the writing of the letter to them. What does he mean by "stability of faith?

> According to the pastor of the First Baptist Church in Greenbrier, Arkansas, Nathan Washburn (a native of Martin, TN), stability of faith means being "...steadfast, loyal, unswayed, fixed, firm, immovable, grounded in the Word of God, strong, having Godly convictions, faithful to the Lord in complete obedience in all areas of our lives."

https://ms-my.facebook.com/faithbaptistgb/videos/maintaining-spiritual-stability-colossians-25-7/1081143249421780/

▲ Colossians 2:7 "...having been firmly rooted and now being built up in Him and established in your faith, just as you were instructed, and overflowing with gratitude."

> The establishment of faith referred to in the verse is a legal figure of speech referring to maturity and/or an issue firmly decided.

▲ 1 Thessalonians 3:2 "...and we sent Timothy, our brother and God's fellow worker in the gospel of Christ, to strengthen and encourage you as to your faith."

> We have learned that the quantity of faith is a fixed amount but the verse shows that it can be strengthened and encouraged through the preaching/teaching of the Word, fellowship, and being exercised in more and varied instances.

▲ 1 Thessalonians 3:10 "...as we night and day keep praying most earnestly that we may see your face, and may complete what is lacking in your faith?"

> Again, the faith of a believer is quantitatively complete but it it may grow qualitatively. So in effect the faith of the believer always has room for enhancement.

▲ 1 Thessalonians 5:8 "But since we are of the day, let us be sober, having put on the breastplate of faith and love, and as a helmet, the hope of salvation."

> The Roman warrior's breastplate, made of chain mail or lorica hamata, protected his vital organs. In like manner the breastplate of faith and love is spiritual protection of the believer's spiritual vitality, and must be worn (active) in order to protect. And, as you know, faith appears in Ephesians 6:16 as the shield to fend off the arrows of our enemy. This is added protection of the believer's spiritual potency.

▲ 2 Thessalonians 1:3 "We ought always to give thanks to God for you, brethren, as is only fitting, because your faith is greatly enlarged, and the love of each one of you toward one another grows ever greater."

> Again this verse gives the impression of increase in quantity while the Koine Greek word ὑπεραυξάνω (according to Lightfoot) refers to an inward growth much like the growth rings of a tree which form at the core. As the believer exercises his/her faith he/she becomes more and more spiritually productive and he/she matures. And that "mustard-seed-sized" faith produces a greater crop. (Matthew. 17:20) Joseph Barber Lightfoot (13 April 1828 – 21 December 1889), was an English theologian, Bishop of Durham, and Bible scholar. . https://en.wikipedia.org/wiki/J._B._Lightfoot

▲ 1 Timothy 1:14 "...and the grace of our Lord was more than abundant, with the faith and love which are found <u>in</u> Christ Jesus."

> From Romans 6:23 we know that eternal life is <u>in</u> Christ Jesus our Lord thus we must go <u>to</u> Him in order to receive it and from John 14:6 we know that no one comes to the Father except <u>through</u> Him and the only thing remaining for salvation is that we confess with our mouths that He is Lord and believe in our hearts that God raised Him from the dead. So it makes sense that the needed faith and love would also be in Jesus. This is echoed in 2 Timothy 1:13. From this verse it seems clear that apart from Jesus' provision we would not have effective faith and agape love. [This comes up again in 2 Timothy 1:13.]

▲ 1 Timothy 1:19 "...keeping **faith** and a good conscience, which some have rejected and suffered shipwreck in regard to their **faith**." [i.e. not practicing faith causes spiritual shipwreck]

> Faith is a spiritual asset and is the key to both salvation and a fruitful walk with Christ. We are to cling to it and continuously and actively exercise it in order to accomplish what God has called us to. Not doing so leads to personal apostasy.

▲ 1 Timothy 6:10 "For the love of money is a root of all sorts of evil, and some by longing for it have wandered away from the faith and pierced themselves with many griefs."

> This does not mean that a believer can lose his/her salvation. Here Paul is referring to their walking away from their continuing to "faith" God as their Shepherd/Provider, commonly known as unbelief which embodies disobedience and distrust. This is the antithesis of faith. [If only English had a word "unfaith.."] Love of money is one of the <u>many</u> distractions of life that can erode faith of the believer.

▲ 1 Timothy 6:12 "Fight the good fight of faith; take hold of the eternal life to which you were called, and you made the good confession in the presence of many witnesses."

> Since faith can move mountains it is one of the potent spiritual weapons in the believer's arsenal to contend against oppression and temptation of all kinds. Search out verses to claim and use against these enemies.

▲ 2 Timothy 1:13 "Follow the pattern of the sound words that you have heard from me, in the faith and love that are <u>in</u> Christ Jesus."

> Paul was preaching sound doctrine and the mature believer discerns this through the Spirit and his/her spirit bears witness of this. Once approved, the words are to be acted upon in faith and love. Again we see that faith and love are in Christ Jesus (See again 1 Timothy 1:14 above)

▲ 2 Timothy 2:18 "...men who have gone astray from the Truth saying that the resurrection has already taken place, and they upset the faith of some."

> Our faith rests upon the life, death, burial, resurrection, and ascension of Jesus Christ and the Truth of the gospel offered to us through the Holy Spirit. Any questioning of this has the potential of demoralizing immature believers.

▲ 2 Timothy 2:22 "Now flee from youthful lusts and pursue righteousness, faith, love and peace, with those who call on the Lord from a pure heart."

> The first step is learning exactly what faith is and then it must be <u>actively</u> pursued. [The verb "pursue" can be defined as to seek and employ measures to obtain or accomplish.]

▲ 2 Timothy 3:15 "...and that from childhood you have known the sacred writings which are able to give you the wisdom that leads to salvation through faith which is in Christ Jesus."

> Again: From Romans 6:23 we know that eternal life is in Christ Jesus our Lord, thus we must go to Him in order to receive it and from John 14:6 we know that no one comes to the Father except through Him and the only thing remaining for salvation is that we acknowledge our sins and confess with our mouths that He is Lord and believe in our hearts that God raised Him from the dead. This is echoed in 2 Timothy 1:13.

▲ 2 Timothy 4:7 "I have fought the good fight, I have finished the course, I have kept the faith;"

> The faith of a believer cannot be lost or taken away but it can certainly be neglected. The koine Greek word translated "kept" (τετήρηκα) means to watch over and preserve. Failure to exercise it makes the believer have a fruitless testimony and walk. Keeping the faith requires us to keep our spiritual eyes and heart on the One who led us to it, take instructions from Him, and be intentional in our walk with Him.

▲ Hebrews 10:39 "But we are not of those who shrink back to destruction, but of those who have faith to the preserving of the soul."

> Beginning in vs. 32 the author is encouraging the continued faith endurance of his readers, noting that there is a sure reward awaiting them. Evidently some have "shrunk back" and have incurred spiritual loss (απωλειαν). From the context we see that "keeping-on-keeping-on" in faith preserves the soul. [The word translated "preserves" (πε ρ ι πο ι η σ η) literally means "grooms".] So we can conclude that steadfast faith grooms our souls.

▲ Hebrews 11:1 "Now faith is the assurance of things hoped for, the conviction of things not seen."

> As stated earlier, faith is not a blind leap into the darkness but a confident step into the Light (Jesus, John 8:12) and the faith of the believer is a window into Truth as well as an assurance and conviction that it is so.

▲ Hebrews 11:4 "By faith Abel offered to God a better sacrifice than Cain, through which he obtained the testimony that he was righteous, God testifying about his gifts, and through faith, though he is dead, he still speaks."

> Abel's blood sacrifice was better than his brother's sacrifice because it was based on

what God commanded. (i.e. His Word] Abel's testimony echoes down through the ages as an example for us to obey God through faith. While we may tend to think of faith beginning with Abram, even a casual reading of Hebrews 11: 4-7 dispels that belief.

▲ Hebrews 11:5 "By faith Enoch was taken up so that he would not see death; and he was not found because God took him up; for he obtained the witness that before his being taken up he was pleasing to God."

Enoch was a person of faith (Hebrews 11:5) who walked with God and found very special favor from Him as did Elijah. They were the only two (besides Jesus) who are recorded to have received this unique treatment and the Bible does not tell us the reason but we might speculate that they just were being trained for their role in the last days as the two witnesses. (Don't quote me on this! See Revelation 11)

▲ Hebrews 11:6 "And without faith it is impossible to please Him, for he who comes to God must believe that He is and that He is a rewarder of those who seek Him."

A nonbeliever not "faithing" Jesus would obviously not please God but neither would a believer who does not actively exercise his/ her faith.

▲ Hebrews 11:7 "By faith Noah, being warned by God concerning events as yet unseen, in reverent fear constructed an ark for the saving of his household. By this he condemned the world and became an heir of the righteousness that comes by faith."

It is not clear in Scripture how or when Noah came to know God before He spoke to him in Genesis 6 but since Noah walked with Him it is clear that they were extremely close. Neither do we know whether God spoke audibly or into his mind but Noah heard, recognized His voice, understood, and obediently carried out the instructions concerning the massive ark, his family, and the animals. This is the simple essence of faith; hearing from God and doing what He asks. And, like in many cases, what God requires does not match up with what is logical or reasonable to man. But, as we know, man's logic and reason are totally inadequate in the face of God's wisdom. (See Isaiah 55:8-9)

▲ Hebrews 11:8 "By faith Abraham, when he was called, obeyed by going out to a place which he was to receive for an inheritance; and he went out, not knowing where he was going."

Faith is such an uncomplicated concept since it is simply obeying Truth, and the only Truth comes from God. Even a few in Old Testament times "got it." Much of what we experience in this world is an illusion. We only "see through a glass darkly" (1 Corinthians 13:12). In our present physical form we have an obscure/imperfect vision of reality. Reality is in the Word, the Spirit and in heaven.

▲ Hebrews 11:9 "By faith he (Abraham) lived as an alien in the land of promise, as in a foreign land, dwelling in tents with Isaac and Jacob, fellow heirs of the same promise;"

God introduced Himself to Abram who accepted Him for who He was, listened, heard, and obeyed. Again, this is the simple essence of faith; hearing from God and doing what He asks. God, being omniscient, saw Abram was an amenable vessel who would willingly obey. He expected a lot from him and as he grew in faith as he moved forward on a seemingly strange circuitous journey. [Am I that available?]

▲ Hebrews 11:11 "By faith even Sarah herself received ability to conceive, even beyond the proper time of life, since she considered Him faithful who had promised."

Abraham's wife, Sarah, even though she was initially skeptical, according to this verse she had over the years witnessed God's total faithfulness and ultimately "faithed" His promise of a son in her advanced age.

▲ Hebrews 11:13 "All these died in faith, without receiving the promises, but having seen them and having welcomed them from a distance, and having confessed that they were strangers and exiles on the earth."

As we know, there are things we "faith" God for that materialize immediately while others arrive later or in the hereafter. The Old Testament saints in this verse died still clinging to whatever they were "faithing." With regard to the promised Messiah they knew without a doubt that He would come even like we are convinced that He will return with the clouds. (Revelation 1:7)

▲ Hebrews 11:17 "By faith Abraham, when he was tested, offered up Isaac, and he who had received the promises was offering up his only begotten son;"

Abraham faltered in his early walk of faith with God but by this time in his spiritual growth Abraham knew without a doubt that His Lord was totally worthy of his full trust, and acted accordingly.

▲ Heb 11:29 "By faith they passed through the Red Sea as though they were passing through dry land; and the Egyptians, when they attempted it, were drowned." [God's command-Exodus 14:16]

> Moses demonstrated faith in obeying God's command to raise his staff for the sea to part and the people demonstrated faith by walking through the sea as the sea was parted. [The dry sea bed must have been a great surprise!]

▲ Hebrews 11:30 "By faith the walls of Jericho fell down after they had been encircled for seven days." [God's command in Joshua 6]

> What better test of faith could there be than being promised that if they circled Jericho's tall protective walls for seven days the walls would collapse? Our God is the Specialist of the impossible!

▲ Hebrews 11:31 "By faith Rahab the harlot did not perish along with those who were disobedient, after she had welcomed the spies in peace."

> This is a tricky one since Rahab was a Canaanite and not a Jew but the passage in Joshua makes it clear that she knew of God's exploits on behalf of Israel and feared Him which is the beginning of wisdom (Psalm 111:10, Proverbs 1:7), is to hate evil (Proverbs 8:13, Job: 28:28), is a fountain of life (Proverbs

14:27, leads to life (Proverbs 19:23, invites God's confiding and covenant (Psalm 25:14), allows a secure fortress/refuge (Proverbs 4:26), will lack nothing (Psalm 34:9) brings blessings (Psalm 112:1), is pure, enduring forever (Psalm 119:9), and is the duty of all mankind (Ecclesiastes 12:13).

▲ Hebrews11:33 "who by faith conquered kingdoms, performed acts of righteousness, obtained promises, shut the mouths of lions,"

If faith can move a mountain (Matthew 17:20-21) it can surely do all of that.

▲ Hebrews 11:39 "And all these, having gained approval through their faith, did not receive what was promised," [during their physical lifetimes]

God encourages and always approves faith (Roman 3:22)

▲ Hebrews 12:2 "...fixing our eyes on Jesus, the author and perfecter of faith, who for the joy set before Him endured the cross, despising the shame, and has sat down at the right hand of the throne of God."

God in Christ both created and sustains the faith of the believer.

▲ Hebrews 13:7 "Remember those who led you, who spoke the Word of God to you; and considering the result of their conduct, imitate their faith."

> God has placed faith warriors before us and we are to imitate their faith example. Find a "faither" and "hang" with them.]

▲ James 1:3 "...knowing that the testing of your faith produces endurance." [i.e. when trials arise]

> Untested faith is weak so we must embrace the tests the Lord assigns and allows. [Dare we thank Him for the tests?]

▲ James 1:6 "But he must ask in faith without any doubting, for the one who doubts is like the surf of the sea, driven and tossed by the wind."

> When we ask it must be coupled with a promise from God's Word or His Spirit.

▲ James 2:1 "My brethren, do not hold your faith in our glorious Lord Jesus Christ with an attitude of personal favoritism."

> While the faithful believer is favored we must realize that God's favor is open to all believers who are "prayed up" and filled with (controlled by) the Holy Spirit. (Proverbs 16:5 etc.) [Don't expect a pat on the back for "faithing" because Our Lord expects it!]

▲ James 2:5 "Listen, my beloved brethren: did not God choose the poor of this world to be rich in faith and heirs of the kingdom which He promised to those who love Him?"

> Riches can easily produce self sufficiency but the neediness of the poor can lead to humility and faith.

▲ James 2:14 "What use is it, my brethren, if someone says he has f**aith** but he has no works? Can that **faith** save him?"

> Genuine faith naturally leads to action but the one boasting of his/her faith without any God-directed works is merely trying to please God and/or others and that is vanity (empty) [Ecclesiastes 2:11, 4:4]

▲ James 2:17 "Even so faith, if it has no works, is dead, being by itself."

> Just as agape love is an active spiritual concept and faculty, so is faith.

▲ James 2:18 "But someone may well say, "You have **faith** and I have works; show me your **faith** without the works, and I will show you my **faith** by my works."

> See previous commentary.

▲ James 2:20 "But are you willing to recognize, you foolish fellow, that faith without works is useless?"

See James 2:14 commentary

▲ James 2:22 "You see that **faith** was working with his works, and as a result of the works, **faith** was perfected;"

Exercising faith perfects it and makes it grow qualitatively.

▲ James 2:24 "You see that a man is justified by works and not by faith alone."

Since faith involves action, one is justified by exercising faith. See 2:14

▲ James 2:26 "For just as the body without the spirit is dead, so also faith without works is dead." [See 2:14]

See James 2:14 commentary

▲ James 5:15 "...and the prayer offered in faith will restore the one who is sick, and the Lord will raise him up, and if he has committed sins, they will be forgiven him."

The prayer would claim this promise of healing.

▲  1 Peter 1:5 "...who (believers) are protected by the power of God through faith for a salvation ready to be revealed in the last time."

> God recognizes His Son dwelling within the believer and preserves him/her by His power for the ultimate salvation. *[Remember that salvation is both an immediate result and a secure process – the believer is saved, he/she is being saved, and will be saved]*

▲  1 Peter1:7 "...so that the proof of your faith, being more precious than gold which is perishable, even though tested by fire, may be found to result in praise and glory and honor at the revelation of Jesus Christ;"

> Genuine faith is precious, survives testing, and will be praised/glorified/ and honored when Jesus is finally revealed.

▲  1 Peter 1:9 "...obtaining as the outcome of your faith the salvation of your souls."

> By God's grace through faith results in spiritual salvation.

▲  1 Peter 1:21 "...who through Him are believers in God, who raised Him from the dead and gave Him glory, so that your faith and hope are in God."

> Faith in and through Jesus ushers in spiritual salvation and connects believers forever with God.

▲ 1 Peter 5:9 "So resist him (the evil one), firm in your faith, knowing that the same experiences of suffering are being accomplished by your brothers and sisters who are in the world".

> Firm faith is a wholehearted reliance upon God and His Truth. It is perfectly effective against our enemy's arrows. And it forms a connection between the believer and born again believers everywhere.

▲ 2 Peter 1:1 "Simon Peter, a bond-servant and apostle of Jesus Christ, To those who have **received** (Strong's 2975) a faith of the same kind as ours, by the righteousness of our God and Savior, Jesus Christ:"

> While I try to stay well clear of the debate concerning inborn faith vs. received faith, this verse appears to be strong ammunition for the context camp. But I will leave the wrangling to theologians.

▲ 2 Peter 1:5 "Now for this very reason also, applying all diligence, in your faith supply moral excellence, and in your moral excellence, knowledge,"

> Diligence, moral excellence, and knowledge are our part in the exercise of our faith. We must apply faith diligently, be "prayed up," living a godly life, and possessing and accurately applying the knowledge we have obtained from God's Truth.

▲ 1 John 5:4 "For whoever is born of God overcomes the world; and this is the victory that has overcome the world— our faith."

> Whether our faith was inborn or granted at rebirth it is unquestionably victorious over manipulation and spiritual mastery by the world system and people of the world when exercised properly because it is based on God's Truth.

▲ Jude 1:3 "Beloved, while I was making every effort to write you about our common salvation, I felt the necessity to write to you appealing that you contend earnestly for the faith which was once for all **delivered to the saints."**

> This verse is yet more evidence supporting the Context Camp's contention that when a person sees the Truth of the gospel, senses a divine calling to be right with God that faith is delivered at that point making it possible to be saved by grace through that faith. As we have seen, "So then <u>faith comes by hearing, and hearing by the Word of God."</u>

▲ Jude 1:20 "But you, beloved, building yourselves up on **your most holy faith**; praying in the Holy Spirit;"

> The Context Camp would debate: "Can inborn faith be holy?" Holy faith is within the Spirit

of Jesus Who is within the believer, so it is His faith that is holy and accessible to the believer.

▲ Revelation 2:13 "'I know where you dwell, where Satan's throne is; and you hold fast My name, and did not deny **My faith** even in the days of Antipas, My witness, My faithful one, who was killed among you, where Satan dwells."

Zeus who was the main Olympian god. But believers in Pergamum were steadfast in faith which the verse identifies as God's faith, yet more ammunition for the Context Camp.

▲ Revelation 14:12 "Here is the perseverance of the saints who keep the commandments of God and their faith in Jesus."

God's commandments cannot be kept apart from faith in Jesus as we walk in His Spirit.

# APPENDIX

## What's It All About, Alfie?

Lyrics:

What's it all about Alfie
Is it just for the moment we live
What's it all about
When you sort it out, Alfie

And if life belongs only to the strong, Alfie
What will you lend on an old golden rule?
As sure as I believe there's a heaven above
Alfie, I know there's something much more

*FINIS*

Printed in the United States
by Baker & Taylor Publisher Services